MW01127157

LIGHTNING
BOLT
BOOKS™

Pembroke Welsh Corgis

Candice Ransom

Lerner Publications • Minneapolis

To my sister, who loves all dogs!

Lerner Publications Company
A division of Lerner Publishing Group, Inc.
241 First Avenue North
Minneapolis, MN 55401 USA

For reading levels and more information, look up this title at www.lernerbooks.com.

Library of Congress Cataloging-in-Publication Data

Names: Ransom, Candice F., 1952- author.
Title: Pembroke Welsh corgis / Candice Ransom.
Description: Minneapolis : Lerner Publications, [2019] | Series: Lightning bolt books. Who's
     a good dog? | Audience: Age 6-9. | Audience: K to Grade 3. | Includes bibliographical
     references and index.
Identifiers: LCCN 2018014517 (print) | LCCN 2018018317 (ebook) | ISBN 9781541543447 (eb pdf)
     | ISBN 9781541538610 (lb : alk. paper) | ISBN 9781541545861 (pb : alk. paper)
Subjects: LCSH: Pembroke Welsh corgi—Juvenile literature.
Classification: LCC SF429.P33 (ebook) | LCC SF429.P33 R36 2019 (print) | DDC 636.737—dc23

LC record available at https://lccn.loc.gov/2018014517

Manufactured in the United States of America
1-45044-35871-6/14/2018

Table of Contents

The Happiest Dog

Look down. See the long, low dog smiling up at you? That's a Pembroke Welsh corgi. Doesn't he look happy?

Corgis have little legs, but nothing slows these pooches down!

Pembroke Welsh corgis are called corgis for short. They stand between 10 and 12 inches (25 and 30 cm) tall. They weigh up to 30 pounds (14 kg).

Corgis are peppy. They are fast learners too. Want your dog to bring your slippers? That's a job for a corgi!

Corgis can be tan, red, brown, or black. They have big heads and pointy ears. They don't need to wag their tails to show they're happy. Their doggy grins give them away.

Corgis often have white markings, and some are several colors.

Work and Play

Dogs can be many different shapes and sizes. The American Kennel Club (AKC) groups dogs by things they have in common. Corgis are in the herding group.

Herding is getting other animals to move as a group.

All herding dogs are good at herding sheep and other animals. They also protect the animals they herd.

The first corgis came from Wales. By day, they herded animals. At night, they watched over their families.

A corgi's big ears pick up any strange sound.

These days, corgis are popular pets. They will do anything to please their owners. It's their new job!

Is a Corgi for You?

Thinking about getting a corgi? Remember the three As: active, alert, and affectionate. Corgis are all of these things.

Active dogs need lots of exercise. A stroll around the block isn't enough. Be ready to walk your corgi for an hour or more each day.

Corgis aren't couch potatoes!

Alert dogs like to stay busy. A bored corgi will get into trouble. Give him toys to chase, dog bones to chew, or even a job to do.

Corgi puppies especially like to chew.

Be sure to spend lots of time with your corgi.

Affectionate corgis love their owners. Your dog will trot along by your side. He'll snuggle up to watch TV. You can always count on your faithful corgi.

Welcome, Corgi!

Happy day! You're bringing your corgi home. You'll also need to bring home doggy supplies. Corgis need bowls, toys, food, and more.

Your corgi needs to see a vet. The vet will check your pooch's health. Ask the vet what you should feed your corgi too.

At home, show your dog his food and water bowls. Keep his water dish filled. Dogs need fresh food and water every day.

Ready to head outside? Snap on your corgi's leash. Get set to have some fun. It's time to explore the world with your new best friend!

Doggone Good Tips!

- Corgis are special. Give your corgi a special name to match. Here are some ideas: Monty, Chester, Duchess, Queenie, or Winston.

- Corgis can get along well with cats. If you have a cat, introduce your corgi slowly. Let the animals sniff each other. Give them time to become friends.

- Corgis love to eat! But don't feed your dog people food. He may love French toast, yet dog food is best for dogs.

Why Corgis Are the Best

- Queen Elizabeth II of Britain owned corgis for years. They had their own room at Buckingham Palace. The sheets on their wicker beds were changed every day.

- Corgis really do smile! Many experts believe that corgis and other dogs raise the corners of their mouths to show happiness, just as people do.

- A corgi's big ears give it a perky look. Corgi puppies have soft, folded ears. Older puppies sometimes have one ear up and one ear down. Up or down, Corgi ears are the cutest!

Glossary

affectionate: feeling or showing a great liking for a person

alert: watchful and quick to act

American Kennel Club (AKC): an organization that groups dogs by breed

herding group: a group of dogs that have a natural ability to control the movement of other animals

peppy: full of energy

vet: a doctor who treats animals

Further Reading

American Kennel Club
http://www.akc.org

American Society for the Prevention of Cruelty to Animals
https://www.aspca.org

Carney, Elizabeth. *Woof! 100 Fun Facts about Dogs.* Washington, DC: National Geographic, 2017.

Fishman, Jon M. *Hero Therapy Dogs.* Minneapolis: Lerner Publications, 2017.

Leighton, Christina. *Pembroke Welsh Corgis.* Minneapolis: Bellwether Media, 2017.

Index

Photo Acknowledgments

Image credits: Independent Picture Service, pp. 2, 22; Rin Seiko/Shutterstock.com, p. 4; Grigorita Ko/Shutterstock.com, p. 5; SawBear/Shutterstock.com, p. 6; Sergieiev/ Shutterstock.com, p. 7; Erik Lam/Shutterstock.com, p. 8; eAlisa/Shutterstock.com, p. 9; steamroller_blues/Shutterstock.com, p. 10; Nadezhda V. Kulagina/Shutterstock.com, pp. 11, 14; everydoghasastory/Shutterstock.com, p. 12; T.Den/Shutterstock.com, p. 13; Mostovyi Sergii Igorevich/Shutterstock.com, p. 15; Bulltus_casso/Shutterstock.com, p. 16; michaeljung/Shutterstock.com, p. 17; Ermolaev Alexander/Shutterstock.com, p. 18; Mostovyi Sergii Igorevich/Shutterstock.com, p. 19.

Cover: Erik Lam/Shutterstock.com.

Main body text set in Billy Infant regular 28/36. Typeface provided by SparkType.